D0288891

THE HUMANNESS OF YOU VOL. II

The Humanness of You Volume II

Poems & Photographs by Walter Rinder

Celestial Arts
Millbrae, Ca 94030

Copyright©1974 by Celestial Arts
231 Adrian Road, Millbrae, California 94030

No part of this book may be reproduced by a any mechanical, photographic, or electronic process, or in the form of a phonographic recording, nor may it be stored in a retrieval system, transmitted, or otherwise copied for public or private use without the written permission of the publisher.

First Printing, June, 1974

Third Printing, September, 1975

Made in the United States of America

Library of Congress Cataloging in Publication Data (Revised)

Rinder, Walter.

The humanness of you.

I. Title.

PS3568.I5H8 811'.5'4 73-86635

ISBN 0-912310-54-5 (v. 2)

Do we give love for giving?
Do we receive love for receiving?
Or are we love
as a flower's fragrance, just is.
Not concerned with a receiver
or a giver.
Just is.

Let us become love.
Let us be love.

from The Humanness of You, Volume I
also available from Celestial Arts

Sonya
whose love asks of me,
be yourself.

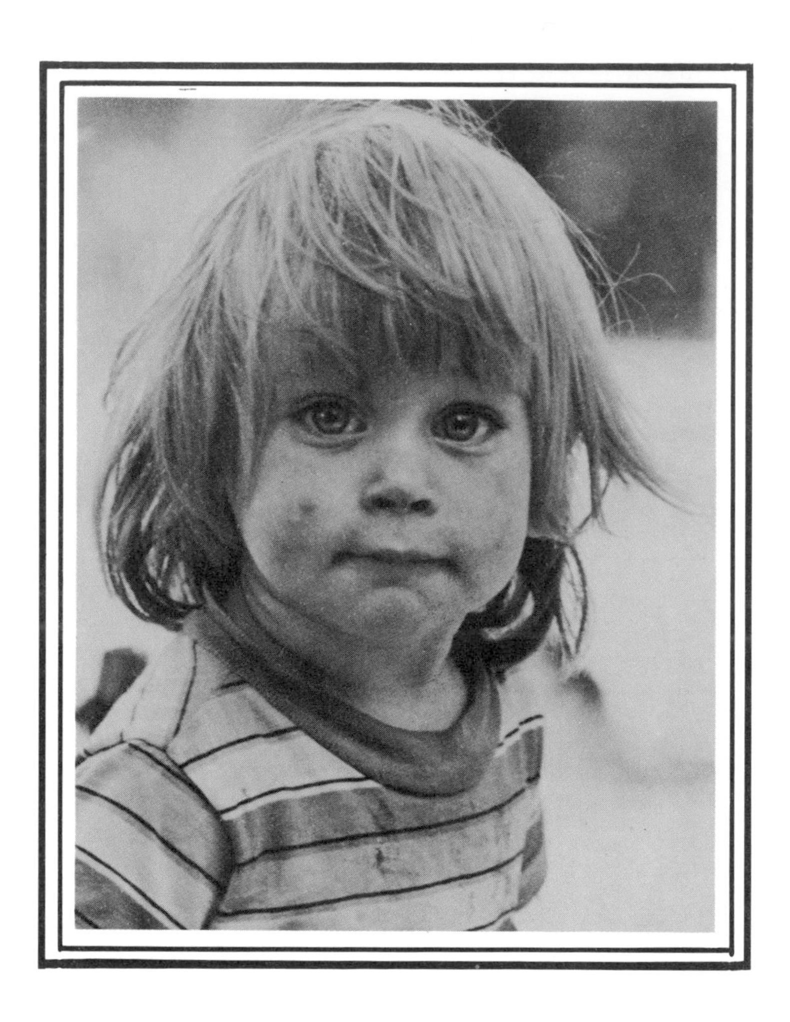

WE ARE OF ALL THINGS

CHILD of now
future
past
CHILD of sun
streams
grass
CHILD of touch
smell
sight
CHILD of day
noon
night
CHILD of black
white
brown
CHILD of words
actions
sounds
CHILD of sister
father
brother
CHILD of innocence
held
by mother
CHILD of skin
face
hair
CHILD of love
standing there

SEEDS OF OUR SOCIETY

a young blond boy wants to hold
a young city girl stands in the cold
a young black girl who longs to share
crying because nobody cares

this is their story of love, not found
as we travel their footsteps upon the ground
from city slums to fertile plains
to ocean harbors to forest rains

they look as far as they can see
when they see what they might be
with naked body in freedoms embrace
the wind says hello as it brushes their face

they ask
are you my friend oh little breeze
will you talk to me oh little trees
man gave me life, I've a soul to share
I'm all alone . . . please . . . please
please someone care

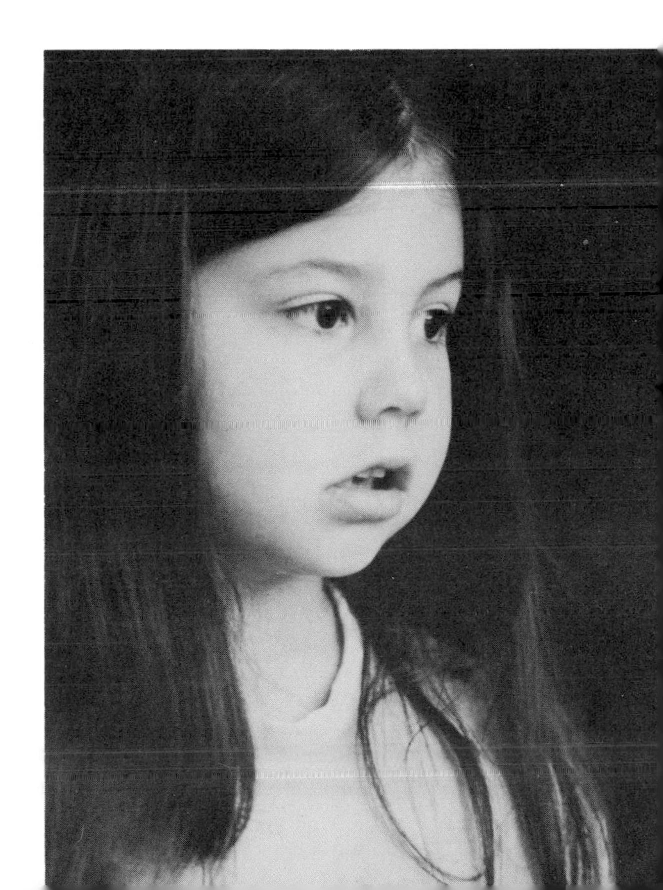

BEGINNINGS

little seeds of the pine
initiate creation
little thoughts of our mind
propagate our nation

little actions and little deeds
grow to become our world, our creed

TO THE CHILDREN

I'll bring you a sky full of blue birds
I'll compose you a rhyme to enjoy
I'll cool your cheeks with a mountain stream
and we'll play with the clouds as our toys

I'll show you the frost in the morning
I'll lead you by day with the sun
I'll guide you to new worlds in the forest
where you can dance and sing and run

I'll share all the trees and wild flowers
all the creatures of this speck of earth
I'll teach you that difference is together
that all love is a part of your birth

I ASKED A MAN

I asked a man
to be my friend
as time passed by he was all pretend

I asked a man
for a place to stay
his uncaring face said, go away

I asked a man
for a cup of tea
he turned his back, ignoring me

I asked a man
to work his farm
my clothes and hair gave him alarm

I asked a man
to share a ride
he said no and passed me by

Into the woods I walked alone
for I had run away from home

His head turned toward the hills—their cover of grain, shortly, would be ready to harvest—then followed the row of trees to where his cabin sat —thinking of the time when the trees were cut, then seasoned, so the walls would be strong and sturdy.

Then his eyes followed the river as it wound itself around the valley and he remembered as a youth the many times the river had wound itself around his life. He never felt alone in this land nor would his family.

THE YOUNG CARPENTER

You asked me what I wanted from life.
Nothing of wealth or fame or great achievements
or to climb mountains or to fly into space.
I wish for a farm, to be close to the earth
so I may watch and help things grow. With a
girl to love and children and be able to give them
simple things like flowers and warm puppies and
fire on winters nights and dreams and wonderment.
Share my knowledge and my love with affection for
all the days and all the nights we are together.
Fill their lives with kindness by listening to what
they feel, and remember, then fill their needs with
those things that make them happy. To mend their
hearts when they are broken and offer strength
when they are in pain. I want to build a home on
simple love.

Graciously yours,

the young carpenter

who smiles a lot

"CAN I WAKE YOU"

May I have a bit of your lifetime,
may I touch you in various ways
with my attitudes and concepts of happiness,
the many experiences we can have in a day.

Can I wake you from your slumber,
present you the colors of green,
may I widen your vision this season
to a way of life you thought but a dream.

"SONYA"

A woman of all the earth; touched by endless compassion, surrounded by the motivation of goodness, moving in and out of lives as the seasons unto one another.

Her beauty is the majesty as I watched the sunset splashing its colors over the Grand Canyon covered by winter's snow, becoming the reality of a dream. Her beauty is the quiet morning hours in Yosemite Valley where I stood as a youth feeling the waves of grass, meadows of smiling wildflowers, cascading waterfalls, high cliffs where I felt I belonged. Those whose breath touches her develop with life's abundance and grow with life's changing tide.

She inspires the most learned of men and the simplest of mind for she knows the woman - - - she is to be.

I love her, not because she is a female, but because she is a woman helping me to become complete in my awareness of love. I love her because she understands those things that confuse my thoughts and hurt my soul. I love her because she asks of me—be yourself.

We were strangers until
I looked your way
my smile said hello
asking you to stay
I'd love to give
this you don't know
until you take the time
so this love I can show

THOSE WONDERFUL PEOPLE

All the rich and joy-filled moments we shared together and the times of solitude we also needed to digest the fullness of human happiness.

The times when our lack of understanding caused us hurt only to be resolved by the security of our love.

Not a day passed in my childhood and youth that you didn't find some way to give even when you were tired or carried a troubled heart.

From you I learned charity and compassion and tolerance. From you I learned to like myself.

I feel your image as a part of me, your lessons mirrored by my deeds.

Mom & Dad, if I suffer or am lonely or feel hurts, it is not because of you, but only that you opened me to so much love I have not yet found a world to give it all to.

MY BROTHERS

Yes, my brothers, I can love you
not just the love within your mind
but also the love your body can give

what meaning has the body
   without a good mind to rule it
what meaning has the mind
   without a body to illuminate it

I UNDERSTAND

I understand I must love myself
  before I can love others.

I understand I must be open
  so I can open others unto themselves.

I understand I must be honest
  if I expect that of my friend.

I understand I must speak the truth
  if I am to hear the truth spoken.

I understand that I must reach out to people
  if I am to be touched.

I understand I must share
  if I am to be given.

I understand my knowledge must be used
  if I am to grow.

I understand you must have freedom
  if I am to be free.

JUSTICE . . .?

the army . . . gave a man a medal for killing another man,
and a dishonorable discharge for
loving one

the state . . . . awarded a man an honor for arresting
men as criminals, and put him in prison
for the criminal act of loving one

the church . . . praised a man for loving mankind,
then condemned him for loving a man

people . . . . . . respect a man's capacity to speak of
love, until he seeks to manifest his words

They marched toward her physical beauty,
drowning out the beauty of her mind. Her
soul beat against the door of her heart waiting
for those who might open that door.

Sex is the result of love
not the cause of love

LEARNING LOVE

I want to learn to love,
It's not something you can teach me,
but its something I can learn from you,
you inspire me
when you tell me how beautiful I am,
that you love me
and you project love also
I begin to look into myself as to why –
you show me myself by being you
I've known you but a short time,
but I trust you –
its a feeling you've given me,
I want to learn by being around you;
Sometimes I feel I want to be
around you forever,
then I realize, as you have told me, that
you're just a stepping stone in my life,
so for me to learn I must not hold back,
help me to learn not to hold back,
help me to learn to love.

I am drunk with happiness
for love has touched me
and will not let go

TIMES WHEN WORDS JUST AREN'T ENOUGH

there are times
when gifts, when money
won't really help
and even kind words of understanding
sound flat and less meaningful

such a time
may be the occasion
when a warm hug
or a touch affection
will have more meaning
will make a deeper impression
upon the heart

if so, give it
without reservation
and feel the beauty
flow both ways.

the path I found a dusty road
beside a garden, freshly hoed

nearby a barn there was a man
a shovel and a smile held in his hand

his hands were calloused, clothes were tattered
his blue eyes glowed with things that mattered

he walked toward me and touched my head
in a moments breath these words he said

these earthy things I wish to share
the work I do, my will to care

I'll be your friend and share my home
love you so you're not alone

I'll show you laughter, tears and joy
I'll be a man, you be a boy

IF THIS WERE YOUR LAST DAY MY SON

If this were your last day, my son,
would you walk upon the sea
to finds the lands beyond your birth
you dreamed someday that you would see.

If this were your last day, my son,
would you write upon the sand
a poem of love your thoughts encased
as death awaits to take your hand.

If this were your last day, my son,
would you see your mother's face
baking cookies in the kitchen
or patching Levi's by the fireplace.

If this were your last day, my son,
would you say to all of man
I'll die not again to propagate
a war, where you have made your stand.

"VISION"

(at the Battleground of Antietam, Virginia)

once there was a cornfield
on a farm near yonder woods
stalks grew strong and golden
as against the sky they stood

farmers working with their plows
lush trees upon the hills
a countryside abundant
from man's sweat, the soil he tilled

the earth began to quiver
twelve thousand men in grey
were marching toward this cornfield
to meet the blue next day

preparations for the battle
were pursued by both the sides
the grey dug earthern trenches
so from bullets they could hide

next morning in the early dawn
the battle had begun
before the ears of ripening corn
felt the warmth of summers sun

through the field the men in blue
charged toward the line of gray
as smoke and powder filled the air
the generals watched and prayed

stalks of corn began to fall
with every bullets thrust
for men and corn became both one
as they fell upon the dust

back and forth the battle raged
on who posessed the field
the blue had it several times
but always had to yield

finally when the darkness came
a peace encased the land
a dying stalk of corn would
represent the body of a man

I gaze upon this solemn place
with fearful eyes I see
a vision of a corn stalk
that my son someday, might be.

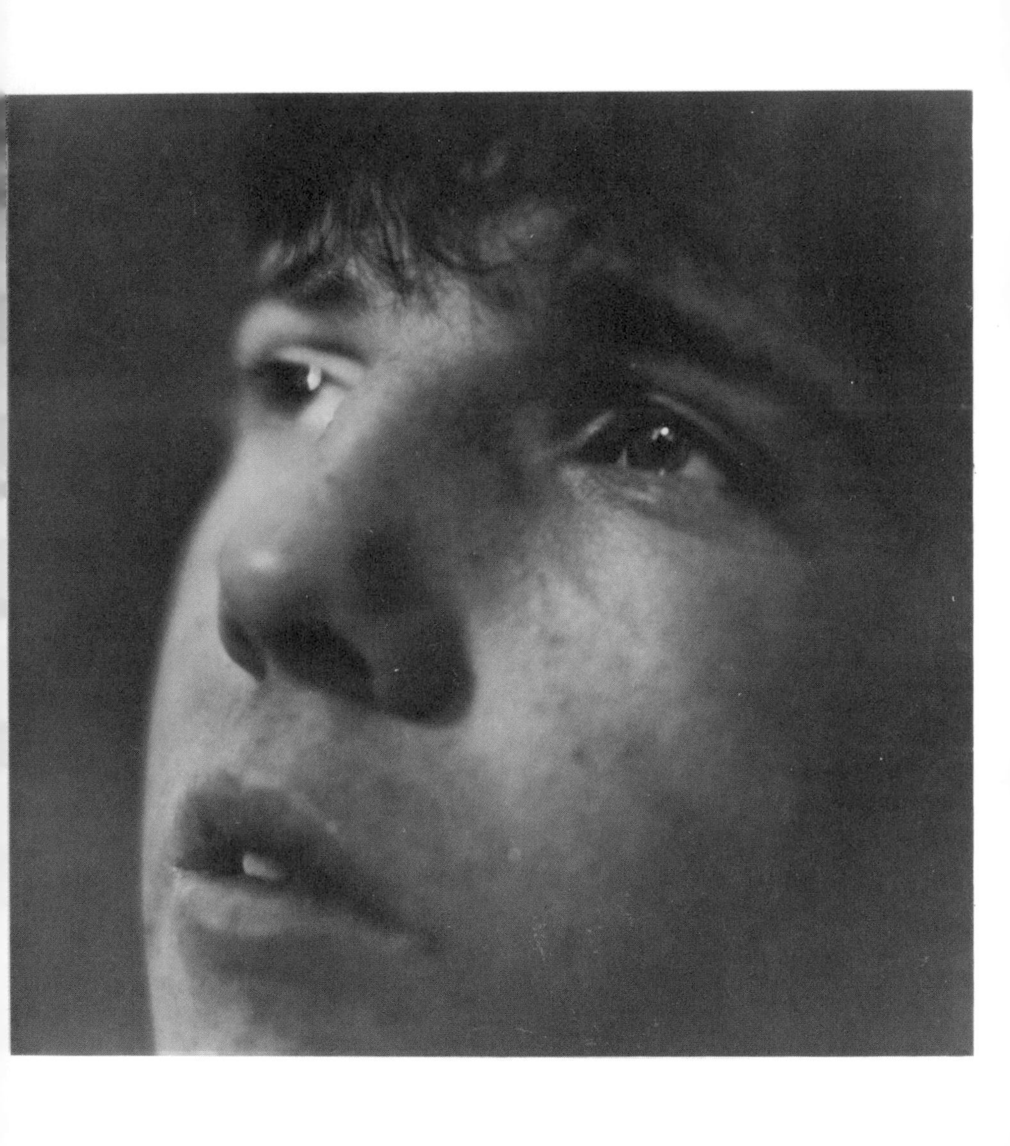

IF I HAD A SON

If I had a son
we'd travel this earth
in search of the truth
a part of his birth

We'd walk, our hands touching
discarding all our fears
that the closeness of love
being together, brings near

I'd give him my knowledge
through experience I've learned
so his life would grow
from those feelings he yearns

I'd give him the clouds
their kisses of rain
when people give hurts
from their fear and their pain

I'd give him the mountains
their snow and their trees
so he could find strength
in the majesty he sees

I'd give him the valleys
their rivers and streams
so his soul could run free
with his fantastic dreams

I'd give him the seasons
so he could see change
developing his thoughts
that nature obtains

I'd give him the day
with the sun and the light
where his body could act
and his senses unite

I'd give him the night
with the moon and the stars
where his mind could wonder
through the universe afar

When he felt the time
his manhood arrived
and he chose to leave
his parents side

I'd be proud and fulfilled
as my hair turned to grey
to know within myself
that we lived every day

that my truth and my sharing
my struggle, my reason to live
was for my son and other youths
that my life's purpose I give

For you God . . . creation
showed my destiny's crown
worn by those souls who search
in themselves where you're found

You're not in heaven or space
or just faith or in dreams
but inside of each human
your truth and love beams

so if I had a son
He'd be touched by your world
that you showed to me
so my love could unfurl

IF A BOY

If a boy is going to be a writer
    he should know how he writes

If a boy is going to be a lawyer
    he should know why he defends

If a boy is going to be a carpenter
    he should know why he builds

If a boy is going to be a philosopher
    he should know why he seeks truth

If a boy is going to be a man
    he should know why he wants to be a man

A MAN

a man . . . acts with honor and pride
yet bends to gather food
for friends in their hunger

a man . . . walks naked
in the forest of his people
so they may see his truth . . .

a man . . . touches all of life
for he is not afraid
to extend himself

a man's . . . work in his labors
shows his love for living

a man . . . is strong and self-confident
yet his eyes may sparkle with rain drops

a man . . . projects the excitement and wonderment
of a child
the experience and understanding
of an adult
upon the screen of life
youth is his audience

A WOMAN

a woman is the calm of a hurricane's eye
where a man finds tranquility
as the storm passes by

a women . . . is the softness inside the shell
when the shell is bombarded
by man's creation of hell

a woman . . .is the pillar of a temple foundation
where a man comes and goes
with renewed inspiration

a woman . . . is the cloud that carries the rain
giving life to man's soul
parched from anxieties and pain

a woman . . . is the bank of the rivers flow
helping man's direction
by being the woman she knows

a woman . . . is the sound of a lark's song in morn
when mist covers life
and man feels forlorn

a woman . . . is the emotion shared with a man
the climax of giving
by the touch of a hand

a woman . . . is the flesh that holds the seed
the miracle of birth
fulfilling human need

a woman . . . is the mother of a new generation
a man is the direction
of that aspiration

THIS SPECK OF EARTH

The man stopped, wiped his brow, scratched
his ear, picked up a stick, raised his head
to look about and saw the long furrows
of his planting. Through the branches he
looked up toward the sunny sky and saw
the rain clouds drifting in from the north
for it was time, the earth was thirsty.

EMOTIONAL CENTER

How long has it been my friend
since we lay aside
our differences
quieted our incessant words
allowing the silent movement
of our feelings
to close the gap, we call
emotion clutter

LEND ME

Lend me room to expand and to grow
Lend me a home where love I can know
Lend me a touch so I can feel
Lend me your time so my hurts can heal
Lend me the freedom to love all men
Lend me the courage to try again and again
I'll give to you a human being whose only intent
Is building life on what you have lent.

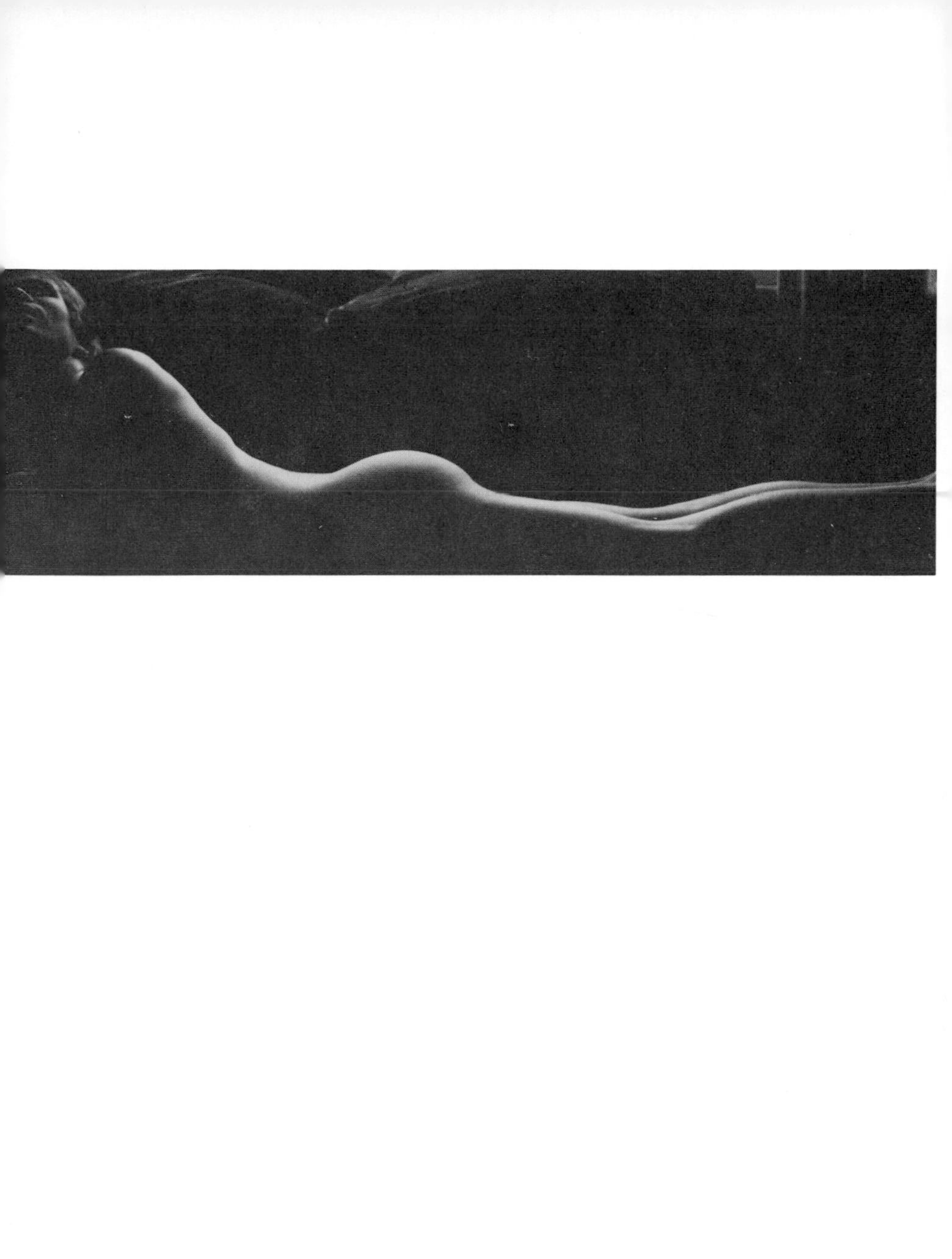

"HUMAN POTENTIAL"

In the time we were together he asked nothing from me beyond a kiss and our embracing one another. I understood him, that he wanted me to know his love was from his soul, not just his body.

I felt comfortable in his company and only wanted to possess what would increase his happiness. I felt a time would come when our bodies would merge as one and our minds would explore, together, the vast reserve of human potential.

THE LOVER OF LOVE

I've seen your face a thousand times . . .
as I remember that week we spent together.
Remembering our walks along the lake when
the night brings people closer together. We
sat by the tall grass and you sang "There's
a place for us. A time and place for us,
peace and quiet and open air".
I will never forget you for you were
one of those rare beautiful human beings who
was gentle and considerate of my feelings
and took the time to make me happy and laughed
with joy when love tickled you.
As the night deepened I felt all life
around us was applauding our involvement.
You who had never learned touching was a sin
nor showing affection was to be feared.

You were the lover of love.

Life speaks to me
it is my heart that listens
not my ears

IF YOU LOSE

If you lose faith in people
        you've lost your chance of sharing
            then someone becomes lonely, besides you

If you lose confidence in yourself
        you've lost your reason of motivation
        then others must supply a vehicle
        if they don't you become stagnant

If you lose consideration of others
        you've lost the respect of yourself
            then ugliness spreads

If you lose your sense of involvement to a cause
                                    or ideal
        you've lost the expansion of your soul
            our world becomes less

If you lose your willingness to labor
        you've lost the growth of yourself
            then you become a leech

If you lose your own thoughts
        you've lost the freedom not to become a slave
                                    you create more masters
            then I must fight harder to maintain
                                        my freedom

If you lose your sense of wonderment, of exploring
of experiencing
you've lost the miracle of learning
then ignorance runs rampant

If you become indifferent
you've lost
we all suffer

CHILDREN OF THE NIGHT

You—oh desert town
dressed
with desert palms
cactus gardens
and desert winds blow
sand across the desert cover
of your streets
money walls of brick and stone
secure your people.
mortared objects
hold your thoughts—in place
pools of gold and silver
caress your appetites
lighted signs, your lamp posts
confuse the serenity
of your star-filled night
darkness empties your
busy streets, crowded sidewalks
your people retiring
to their rich, abundant
materialistic Gods.

Each and every night
from the shadows, emerge

the children of the streets
"street people"
whose short lives
have woven a precious cloak
of warm, protecting fibers
for your displaced youth
who have wandered
to your warm and sunny days
Oh desert town
those whose difference
is distasteful to your kind
those youth whose hardships
is beyond your caring
of lives abused
in body and in mind
of lives whose splints
hold the broken trust
and broken hearts and broken homes
and broken hope
none the less
they find a way
to fill the empty gaps
and find a meaning to their
endless wanderings

by accepting, their differences
as a bond
traveling towns and cities
contemplating
somewhere, sometime
a feeling of belonging
stopping long enough, to build
or reconstruct a reason
to continue searching
for the balance
as a way of life

This special night
four of them came together
this destiny proclaimed
by God alone
under the cover of
a single palm tree
four lives in timeless
awaking or reawaking
shattering barriers
into fragments
souls released
in exploration

one soul cried tears of happiness
upon being born again
one soul enhanced a vision
of himself
one soul realized, in clear thoughts,
her true desires
one soul torn away at the protective
coating of his feelings
then ran away for fear
it was not enough
and would be taken away
as all else had
he loved.
they parted
not the same
as before they met
but with renewed
purpose and direction
realizing
clouds of dispair
may often cover
the warming rays of joy

four youths
standing before a shattered world
beginning to understand
that difference must be shown
through experience, only, is it known
that truth a weapon of the soul
is fought with love
not sword nor twisted tongue
to cut the pieces from the whole

Oh desert town
you tolerate their existence
but if you had the time
or the will of action
to alleviate their presence
on your streets
which mar your image
you would indeed
They no more
could bring to life
the desert nights
as minstrels or story tellers,
with songs of traveled highways
vagabonds of God
they the only people to say
"Hello" and volunteer their
time to me a lonely
stranger to your town.
Your street people
are more real
in searching for truth
than all of you
whose security is
behind your doors
with lock and key

To the

PARENTS . . . ADULTS . . . LEADERS OF SOCIETY

Kids fight for everykindness
Kids fight through every day
We run over human beings
when they happen in our way.

Kids fight for coexistence
Kids fight against money's gain
We tamper with the human soul
supressing criticizing . . . complain

Can't you see how you are living
Can't you stop and think?
take a look around you
find those missing links

that will change your son or daughter
or help kids on our streets
give them a chance to live
with love, so they can meet

you . . . a person they can honor
you . . . a person they can feel
create pride with your years of knowledge
give them strength and with kindness seal

their confidence—you have shattered
their caring—you have crushed
the love you never showed them
your time was always rushed.

Youth, our hopes, our dreams, our future
in our destiny, they stand.
"You are responsible" with your actions
lay down your swords

REACH OUT YOUR HAND

A WAY OF LIFE

searching for a way of life
can be your richest accomplishment
involving all emotions
encompassing basic needs
not only for survival
but for the entire spectrum of love
lasting a lifetime

searching for only moments
of happiness and pleasure

lead to loneliness, despair
and small amounts of awareness
of yourself

ONE OF A KIND

you
unique
a wonderful addition to life
   for there is no one else like you

you are important
believe it . . . know it
allow your realization
to radiate among
your fellow man
   for there is no one else like you

reflect your feelings
your hopes . . . your dreams
you have much to contribute
take your time
don't hurry
tomorrow will wait for you
   for there is no one else like you

grow with your difference
be proud . . . be happy
like yourself
become a new experience
for other people
they can learn from you
  for there is no one else like you

the world needs you
when you hold back
the world is that much less
  for there is no one else like you

may this night find you at peace with yourself. Close your eyes and in your sleep, this night, dream once more of finding love and a way of life. For tomorrow begins another unknown journey into the world of a new day.

Allow people to know of you
of your humanness

rejoice
for without hope and dreams
what freedom is secure

ABOUT THE AUTHOR

Instead of writing an autobiography in this book, as I have done in my other books, I would rather ask you to share your feelings with me, as I have done with you.

You may write to me –

Walter Rinder
c/o This Speck of Earth Gallery
315 S.W. Morrison
Portland, Oregon 97204

My life has been a question: Is it practical for the modern individual to follow his feelings, or is that an idealistic notion, completely unattainable?

Despite all opposition, we must maintain strength in our own belief – the strong feeling that we must not allow others to imprison our spirit through their own forceful actions.

I treasure my right to be myself and want, through this book, to share it with you, knowing that as my capacity for self-expression expands, I follow my feelings to a way of life, so perhaps will you.

Walter Rinder

OTHER BOOKS by Walter Rinder

Love is an Attitude
This Time Called Life
Spectrum of Love
Follow Your Heart
The Humanness of You – Vol. 1
Only One Today
My Dearest Friend
Love Is My Reason
Will You Share With Me?

CELESTIAL ARTS BOOK LIST

LOVE IS AN ATTITUDE. The world-famous book of poetry and photographs by Walter Rinder. 128 pages, clothbound. $7.95; paperbound, $3.95.

THIS TIME CALLED LIFE. Poetry and photography by Walter Rinder. 160 pages, clothbound, $7.95; paperbound, $3.95.

SPECTRUM OF LOVE. Walter Rinder's remarkable love poem with magnificently enhancing drawings by David Mitchell. 64 pages, clothbound, $7.95; paperbound, $2.95

FOLLOW YOUR HEART. A new and powerful companion to the fabulously successful Spectrum of Love with illustrations by Richard Davis. 64 pages, clothbound, $5.95. paperbound, $2.95.

THE HUMANNESS OF YOU. Walt Rinder philosophy and art rendered in his own words and photographs. 64 pages, paperbound, $2.95.

GROWING TOGETHER. George and Donni Betts' poetry with photographs by Robert Scales. 128 pages, paperbound, $3.95.

VISIONS OF YOU. Poems by George Betts, with photographs by Robert Scales. 128 pages, paperbound, $3.95.

MY GIFT TO YOU. New poems by George Betts, with photographs by Robert Scales. 128 pages, paperbound, $3.95.

YOU & I. Leonard Nimoy, the distinguished actor, blends his poetry and photography into a beautiful love story. 96 pages, clothbound, $7.95; paperbound, $2.95.

SPEAK THEN OF LOVE. Deep and sensitive poems from Andrew Oerke with beautifully illustrated drawings from ancient Asian texts. 80 pages, paperbound, $3.95.

WILD BIRDS AND OTHERS. Poetry rich in imagry and depth of compassion from Wendy Long. Beautiful photographs by Ron Sugiyama. 80 pages, paperbound, $2.95

WHERE DO YOU GO FROM HERE? Poignant, funny, always moving, one-liners in a circus of photographs by Robert Weston. 64 pages, paperbound, $2.95.

I AM. Concepts of awareness in poetic form by Michael Grinder. Illustrated in color by Chantal. 64 pages, paperbound, $2.95.

SONG TO THEE, DIVINE ANDROGYNE (Seven Steps to Heaven). A Psalm of Praise for the new age integrating modern psychology with ancient religion by Rowena Pattee. 128 pages, paperbound, $3.95.

GAMES STUDENTS PLAY (And what to do about them.) A study of Transactional Analysis in Schools, by Kenneth Ernst. 128 pages, clothbound, $7.95; paperbound, $3.95.

A GUIDE FOR SINGLE PARENTS (Transactional Analysis for People in Crisis.) T.A. for single parents by Kathern Hallett. 128 pages, clothbound, $7.95; paperbound, $3.95.

THE PASSIONATE MIND (A Manual for Living Creatively with One's Self.) Guidance and understanding from Joel Kramer. 128 pages, paperbound, $3.95.

DREAMS: Messages From My Self. A sensitive effort aimed at helping individuals appreciate and interpret their own dreams by Ruth Kramer. 80 pages, paperbound, $2.95.

THE SENSIBLE BOOK (A Celebration of Your Five Senses.) Barbara Polland awakens the understanding of their senses for children. 64 pages, paperbound, $3.95.

THE LIBERATED MOTHER GOOSE. A bold stroke in behalf of the re-education of children and their parents from Tamar Hoffs. 128 pages, paperbound, $3.95.

THE SPORTS TIME MACHINE. Newslike text and pictures of the great moments in the history of sports by Dave Brase and Tim Simons. 90 pages, paperbound, $2.95.